Our Love & Blessings Jean

Dot & Jim

THE KATHLEEN PARTRIDGE SERIES

Kathleen Partridge's Book of Flowers
Kathleen Partridge's Book of Friendship
Kathleen Partridge's Book of Golden Thoughts
Kathleen Partridge's Book of Tranquil Moments


First published in Great Britain in 1997 by
Jarrold Publishing Ltd
Whitefriars, Norwich NR3 1TR

Designed and produced by Visual Image, Craigend, Brimley Hill,
Churchstanton, Taunton, Somerset TA3 7QH

Illustrations by Jane Watkins

Edited by Donald Greig

ISBN 0-7117-0903-3

Copyright © Jarrold Publishing 1997

Printed by Proost, Belgium 1/97

# Kathleen Partridge's
## BOOK OF
# Golden Thoughts

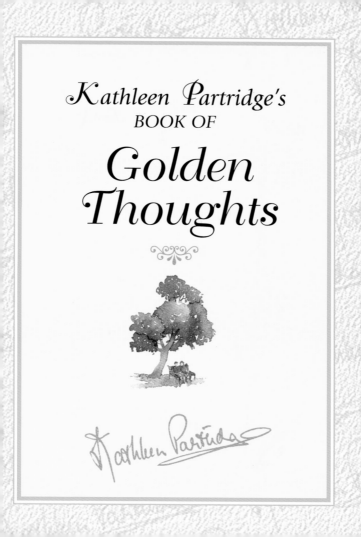

# Smiling Along

Roaming the byways outside the great city,
The sky seems too large for my little concerns,
Worries are lost in the green of the landscape,
A sense of wellbeing and wonder returns.

A good wholesome breeze sweeps the frowns
from my forehead,
Here is simplicity, fragrant and free;
It is enough to be living this minute,
To feel and to hear; to think and to see.

My values of living take on a fresh aspect
With every green leaf that I notice unfurled.
Roaming the byways is good as a tonic,
I come home renewed to the work-a-day world.

# Steadfast

Be thankful for the loving heart
That always stays the same,
The one who stands beside you
Sharing failure, fun or fame

Whose ways will never alter
Whose eyes will always smile
Even though you haven't been
So cheerful for a while.

One who loves you just as much
Though happy or depressed
In sickness or in health
When at your worst or at your best.

# God Bless You

'God bless you.' There's no other
greeting quite so fond as this,
No sweeter phrase for meeting, or to
speed the parting kiss.

No other words convey so much
sincerity of heart,
For when the guests arrive or when
the loyal friends depart.

No sentence is more suitable or has a
truer ring
Than this sweet phrase 'God bless
you', for it covers everything.

# Good Wishes

To wish you 'Good Morning', the sun on the lattice,
To give you sweet thought, sing the birds in the trees,
To bring you bright wisdom, the dew on the flowers,
With peace for your vision and joy for your ease.

Perfume at twilight to comfort your dreaming,
Quiet at sundown when shadows descend,
A stream with a melody lapping a lullaby,
Good wishes, Good night and God bless you, my
friend.

# Rainbows in the Sky

Why does the sun pierce the mists of the morning?
Why does a rainbow smile out of the rain?
Why does the silver line cling to the billows
And earth after storms have a joyful refrain?

Just as a proof that the dark days are passing
That shadows are made by the light of the sun,
That life may look black for the space of a season
But there is a rainbow for everyone.

# Bright Day

I'll think of something bright today
as I commence my work,
I'll bring out all my memories where
happy moments lurk.

I'll carry on my lips a song that has
a cheeky tune,
I will be brisk and bright and do my
duties twice as soon.

I won't be disappointed with the
vagaries of fate,
And if one plan should fail, I'll make
another soon, or late.

*Little things shall please me, setbacks
shall not make me cross,
I'll laugh when I'm in luck and find
philosophy for loss.*

*I'll wake up with a smile today at
life's insistent call,
Come rain, or shine, my heart is big
enough to take it all.*

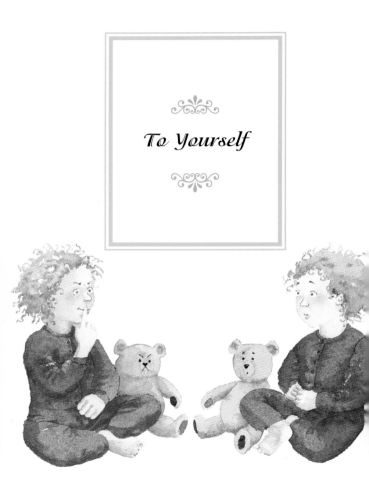

To Yourself

*Stand beside yourself sometimes and get*
*another view;*
*Try to see yourself the way an onlooker*
*might do;*
*Recognise a habit, mark a weakness or a*
*groove;*
*There is no better way to help yourself*
*and to improve.*

*Set yourself a standard, have an ideal in*
*your mind;*
*Any deed beneath your standard you*
*must leave behind;*
*Be your own observer, knowing what*
*you must surmount,*
*And to your heart and conscience every*
*day give an account.*

# Always Peace

This is the place, this dell of greens and browns,
Where summer dwells and bluebells don their
gowns;
Where squirrels organise their busy day,
And swallows call before they fly away;
Where daffodils dance round the roots of trees,
And creepers ramble anywhere they please.

Not even words like 'peace' and 'sweet content'
Are deep enough where views are heaven sent;
For this green dell no turmoil ever knows
From spring's fair birthright through to winter
snows;
Here beauty lives and gentleness has grown,
And what is 'peace' where nothing else is known?

Best Wishes

I wish for you, when you are old, a
cottage garden small and free,
A crazy path between the flowers, a
seat beneath an apple tree.

I wish for you a fond relation or a
very loyal friend,
Some lovely memories to gather when
the day is at an end.

I wish for you a quiet wisdom that
will counteract small fears,
But most of all a happy heart that
never ages with the years.

# To a Friend

A golden thought has just begun
Where flowers blossom in the sun
And rivers sing to those who pass
While shadows lean against the grass.

Then I would wish a friend like you
Another friend as good and true
To share the road of life's design
With humour and a love divine.

# Sunbeams

If all the golden sunbeams
Could be gathered in to spend
With all the loving thoughts and deeds
When day was at an end

And tied with strings of laughter
On wings of wonder born
They'd beautify the eventide
And bless tomorrow's dawn.

# Toll of Time

Time takes its toll
And those we love grow dearer with the years,
Of no avail are past regrets
Life has no time for tears.

Live and laugh and help each other
Whether working or at leisure,
To be happy, loved and needed
Is life's greatest source of pleasure.

# River of Life

Peace and the flowing river of life
Offer us hope and a little song,
A sense of comfort and ease from strife
Whenever the toils of life are strong.

And over the hills where the views are kind
A feeling of freedom is waiting there,
A solace of heart and soul and mind
Out on the grass in the open air.

# Dream Cottage

We picture a country cottage
Set in a country lane
Scented with old fashioned flowers
And sheltered against the rain.

Old timbers and quiet windows
With a beautiful garden view
Where the shadows play in the evening
And the morning sun filters through.

It's a dream that can make us happy
When we live in a busy part
Dreaming the dream of 'Our Cottage'
And keeping the hope in our heart.

## Blossoming Smile

Nature's loveliness would pall
If flowers had no scent at all,
For beauty lifeless stands apart
Without the fragrance in the heart.

A maiden might a goddess be
Perfect in grace and symmetry,
Yet stand unnoticed for a while
Without the beauty of a smile.

# *For Old Time's Sake*

*Think golden thoughts
And send out gentle blessings
Offer a prayer
Each time you look above.*

*For kindly people
Found in pleasant places
Remember them, for old time's sake,
With love.*

# Top of the Hill

I'd always live at the top of the hill
Looking out at a beautiful scene,
I'd always live where the air is fresh
And the roads are pleasant and green,
But if I can't live at the top of the hill
I'll live looking up and not down.

And if I must dwell in a crowded part
And walk through a dusty town,
I'll look for the sun in the ways of men
And for space in a mind that is broad;
I'll watch for fragrance in human lives
And in hearts, for peace and concord.

Looking up and not down,
Looking forward, not back –
And there will be magic still
In the seeking and finding of beauty in life –
Just as if I live up on the hill.